America in the 1960s and 1970s

By
CINDY BARDEN

COPYRIGHT © 2002 Mark Twain Media, Inc.

ISBN 1-58037-215-5

Printing No. CD-1561

Mark Twain Media, Inc., Publishers
Distributed by Carson-Dellosa Publishing Company, Inc.

Table of Contents

1 About the American History Series
2 A Decade of Challenge and Change
3 A New Decade Begins: 1960
4 The Presidential Election of 1960
5 Russians Lead the Space Race in 1961
6 President John F. Kennedy
7 What Was New in '62?
8 Silent Spring
9 ZIP into 1963
10 Dr. Martin Luther King, Jr.
11 I Have a Dream
12 The Assassination of the President
13 What Happened in 1964?
14 President Lyndon B. Johnson
15 Civil Rights Laws Passed
16 If You Were Alive in '65
17 United States Involved in a No-Win War
18 "Beam Me Up, Scotty"
19 Tune In, Turn On, Drop Out
20 Sixties Scavenger Hunt
21 What Happened in 1967?
22 Then and Now
23 1968: A Turbulent Year
24 Environmental Awareness
25 In the News in 1969
26 President Nixon's First Term
27 To the Moon—and Back
28 Can You Tell Me How to Get to Sesame Street?
29 Who's Who?
30 Fashions in the Sixties

31 Jeopardy!
32 The 1970s
33 What Happened in 1970?
34 Pop Goes the Art World
35 In the News in 1971
36 Headline News
37 What Was New in '72?
38 What Was Watergate?
39 Prices Rose in 1973
40 The Second Battle of Wounded Knee
41 The President Resigns
42 Meet Gerald R. Ford
43 Ford Grants Pardons in 1974
44 What Happened in 1975?
45 How Things Have Changed
46 That's a Big Ten-Four, Good Buddy (1976)
47 Computers Come of Age
48 What Happened in 1977?
49 What If?
50 News in '78
51 Math Facts
52 President Jimmy Carter
53 Hostages Taken in 1979
54 What Was New?
55 Seventies Scavenger Hunt
56 Read All About It
57 The 1970s Newbery Award Winners
58 History Projects
59 Learn More About ...
60 Suggested Reading
61 Answer Keys

About the American History Series

Welcome to *America in the 1960s and 1970s,* one of the books in the Mark Twain Media, Inc., American History series for students in grades four to seven.

The activity books in this series are designed as stand-alone material for classrooms and home-schoolers or as supplemental material to enhance your history curriculum. Students can be encouraged to use the books as independent study units to improve their understanding of historical events and people.

Each book provides challenging activities that enable students to explore cultural, historical, geographical, and social studies topics. The activities provide research opportunities and promote critical reading, thinking, and writing skills. As students learn about the people and events that influenced history, they will draw conclusions; write opinions; compare and contrast historical events, people, and places; analyze cause and effect; and improve thinking skills. Students will also have the opportunity to apply what they learn to their own lives through reflection and creative writing.

Students can further increase their knowledge and understanding of historical events by using reference sources at the library and on the Internet. Students may need assistance to learn how to use search engines and discover appropriate websites.

Titles of books for additional reading appropriate to the subject matter at this grade level are included at the end of the book.

Although many of the questions are open-ended, answer keys are included for questions with specific answers.

Share a journey through history with your students as you explore the books in the Mark Twain Media, Inc., American History series.

Discovering and Exploring the Americas
Life in the Colonies
The American Revolution
The Lewis and Clark Expedition
The Westward Movement
The California Gold Rush
The Oregon and Santa Fe Trails
Slavery in the United States
The American Civil War
Abraham Lincoln and His Times
The Reconstruction Era
Industrialization in America
The Roaring Twenties and Great Depression
World War II and the Post-War Years
America in the 1960s and 1970s
America in the 1980s and 1990s

Name: _____ Date: _____

A Decade of Challenge and Change

The 1960s were a decade of challenge, change, and turmoil in the United States. During the 1950s, the relationship with communist countries had been very stormy. The Cold War was very much a reality when the 1960s began, and many feared the situation would soon get worse.

As relations with Cuba and the Soviet Union deteriorated, Americans reacted to their fear of a nuclear war by building backyard fallout shelters, which they stocked with canned goods, drinking water, first aid kits, and other supplies. They needed to believe they could find safety in the event the United States was hit by a nuclear bomb.

The population of the United States was at 179,245,000 in 1960. The average weekly salary was $89.72. Ninety percent of American homes had television sets, but it wasn't until 1967 that sales of color TV sets outnumbered black-and-white models.

The Space Age began with spacecraft orbiting Earth. By the end of the decade, the first men had set foot on the moon.

People sang to folk music and danced to rock-and-roll. They welcomed The Beatles and other British rock groups. Elvis Presley had three of the top single hits for 1960 and remained a top seller for the entire decade.

Hippies and drugs made the scene. "Flower children" preached love and peace as they explored alternative lifestyles.

Women wore their skirts shorter; men wore their hair longer.

Millions of protestors showed their support for civil rights and their nonsupport for the war in Vietnam. Some gains in civil rights were achieved, but the war in Southeast Asia showed no signs of ending by the end of the decade.

The women's liberation movement gained momentum with the theme "Equal pay for equal work."

In his acceptance speech as the Democratic candidate for president in 1960, John Kennedy stated, "We stand at the edge of a New Frontier, the frontier of the 1960s ... Beyond that frontier are uncharted areas of science and space, unsolved problems of peace and war, unconquered pockets of ignorance and prejudice, unanswered questions of poverty and surplus." Kennedy challenged Americans to become "new pioneers of that New Frontier."

1. What "new frontiers" do you think people face today?

_____

_____

_____

_____

Name: _____ Date: _____

A New Decade Begins: 1960

- An electronic larynx provided voice communication for people who could not talk.

- *Tiros I* became the first weather satellite.

- The Post Office began experimenting with fax mail.

- Zenith™ tested subscription TV but found it unsuccessful.

- Parker™ introduced a fountain pen with refill cartridges. (Ballpoint pens were still in the future.)

- Mattel's™ Chatty Cathy doll spoke 11 phrases in random order.

- The ATM was invented by Luther Simjian in 1960.

- New at the movies: Smell-O-Vision. Moviegoers weren't impressed.

- An American rocket launched from Cape Canaveral, Florida, strayed off course in November, crashing on the island of Cuba. The only casualty—one cow was killed. The Cuban government used the "tragedy" to embarrass the United States. They gave the cow an official funeral and paid tribute to it as a victim of the United States' "imperialist aggression."

The top television programs this year were "Gunsmoke," "Wagon Train," "Have Gun, Will Travel," "The Danny Thomas Show," and "The Real McCoys."

1. Use the Internet and other reference sources. What do the initials ATM stand for?

   _____

2. Do you think you would have enjoyed movies with Smell-O-Vision? Why or why not?

   _____

   _____

   _____

   _____

3. What do you think of the reaction by the Cuban government to the "tragedy" of the cow's death?

   _____

   _____

   _____

   _____

Name: _____ Date: _____

The Presidential Election of 1960

The two major candidates for the presidential election of 1960 were John F. Kennedy and Richard M. Nixon. Both became president: Kennedy in 1961 and Nixon in 1969. Decide which president each statement refers to. Write RN (for Nixon), JFK (for Kennedy), or BOTH (for statements that apply to both) on the lines before the statements. Use the Internet or other reference sources if you need help.

_____ 1. Born in 1913.

_____ 2. Born in 1917.

_____ 3. Illnesses during childhood forced him to spend long periods of time in bed.

_____ 4. Served 14 years in Congress as representative and senator.

_____ 5. Served 8 years as Vice President of the United States.

_____ 6. Underwent several operations for back problems and often needed crutches to walk.

_____ 7. Religion: Catholic

_____ 8. Religion: Quaker

_____ 9. Graduated second in his class from Whittier College and third in his class from Duke University Law School.

_____ 10. While in college, he joined the debate team, acted in school plays, and sang in the Glee Club.

_____ 11. While in college, he played football and was a member of the swim team.

_____ 12. A serious student in college, he spent so many hours at his desk studying that his classmates nicknamed him "Iron Butt."

_____ 13. Joined the navy during World War II.

_____ 14. Democratic candidate

_____ 15. Republican candidate

For the first time, two presidential candidates met for a series of four televised debates. On camera, Kennedy appeared calm and confident. In contrast, Nixon seemed pale and nervous.

Even though Kennedy outshone his opponent in the debates, the election was close. When the votes were counted, Kennedy had won by a narrow margin in popular votes.

Name: _____ Date: _____

Russians Lead the Space Race in 1961

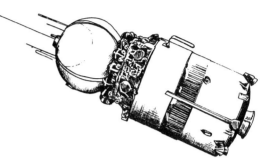

- The Russian astronaut, Yuri Gagarin, became the first man to orbit Earth on April 12, 1961. The United States wasn't far behind in the "space race." Less than a month later, the U.S. space-craft *Freedom 7* carried astronaut Alan Shepard into space.

- Time-Life Books™ began publication.

- IBM's Shoebox™, an early computer, could recognize 16 voice commands and do simple arithmetic.

- The FCC approved FM stereo broadcasting.

- Two new shows, "Ben Casey" and "Dr. Kildare," began a popular type of TV series, the medical drama.

- President Kennedy appointed Dr. Janet G. Travell as the first woman to hold the post of personal physician to the president.

- John F. Kennedy presented the first live presidential news conference from Washington, D.C.

- In his inaugural address on January 20, 1961, John F. Kennedy inspired a new wave of patriotism with the words, "Ask not what your country can do for you; ask what you can do for your country."

- He must have been "smarter than the average bear" because in 1961 Yogi Bear got his own cartoon series.

Use the Internet or other reference sources if needed.

After nine years as a radio series, "Gunsmoke" moved to television with James Arness as marshal.

1. On your own paper, write what you think JFK meant in his inaugural speech.

2. What do the initials FCC and FM stand for?

   _____

   _____

3. Where did Yogi Bear live? _____

Name: _____ Date: _____

President John F. Kennedy

John F. Kennedy accomplished much in his short time as president. He strongly promoted the U.S. space program; held peace talks with Russian leader, Nikita Khrushchev; proposed a stop to the testing of atomic weapons in the atmosphere; and arranged for a nuclear test ban treaty.

While president, John F. Kennedy established the Peace Corps, an organization that sent people and supplies to needy countries. Over the years, thousands of volunteers have helped plant crops, dig wells, build schools, and improve standards of living.

Shortly after becoming president, Kennedy approved a plan by the Central Intelligence Agency (CIA) to train Cuban exiles and help them plan a return to Cuba to overthrow Fidel Castro, the communist leader. American boats landed the anti-Castro troops on a beach called the Bay of Pigs. The troops were greatly outnumbered, and the revolution was a disaster.

Berlin, Germany, was divided after World War II. In August 1961, the Communists built a 25-mile wall of concrete and barbed wire across the middle of the city to prevent people in East Berlin from leaving.

In a speech in Berlin, Kennedy stated: "Freedom has many difficulties, and democracy is not perfect, but we have never had to put up a wall to keep our people in."

The United States had its own difficulties with freedom at that time, and many "invisible walls" had been built to keep Blacks and women from exercising the same freedoms available to White males.

Lack of civil rights for Blacks, especially in the South, led to protests, riots, and violence. Addressing the problem, Kennedy stated: " ... this nation, for all its hopes and all its boasts, will not be fully free until all its citizens are free."

1. Do you think the United States should help people in other countries overthrow a leader they do not like? Why or why not?

   _____

   _____

   _____

2. Do you believe all citizens of the United States are now truly free? Why or why not?

   _____

   _____

   _____

Name: _____ Date: _____

What Was New in '62?

- **New TV programs:** "The Jetsons" and "The Beverly Hillbillies."

- **New member:** Jackie Robinson, the first Black player in the major leagues, was inducted into the Baseball Hall of Fame.

- **New fears:** The U.S. State Department denied passports to American citizens who were members of the Communist Party.

- **New problems:** An unmanned spaceship launched to provide the first close-up view of Venus crashed four minutes after take-off. The problem, caused by a minor error made by a computer programmer, cost the U.S. space program $18.5 million.

- **New style:** Touch-tone phones were featured at the Seattle World's Fair.

- **New heights:** John Uelses became the first pole-vaulter to jump 16 feet indoors.

- **New stores:** K-Mart and Wal-Mart opened their first stores.

- **New way to communicate:** The Telstar satellite, launched in 1962, was the first international communication satellite to transmit transatlantic images for television.

- **New frontiers:** Astronaut John Glenn became the first American to orbit Earth in the *Friendship 7* space capsule.

- **New rules:** The U.S. Supreme Court ordered that James Meredith, a Black student, be admitted to the all-White University of Mississippi.

- **New team:** The New York Mets became a National League baseball team this year. They were originally named the Metropolitans.

Use the Internet or other reference sources to answer the following questions.

1. Use a dictionary. Define *transatlantic*.

   _____

2. How do you think you would have felt if you had been James Meredith?

   _____

   _____

3. Why do you think the Metropolitans' name was quickly changed to the Mets?

   _____

Name: _____ Date: _____

Silent Spring

Marine biologist Rachel Carson was the first to alert the public to the grave environmental consequences of the use of DDT and other pesticides. Her book, *Silent Spring*, published in 1962, issued a call to action by warning that pesticides were a danger not only to wildlife but also to people.

In the 1950s, pesticides, especially DDT, were heavily used in many parts of the world to kill disease-carrying and crop-eating insects. The results seemed very beneficial at first as the number of cases of yellow fever, typhus, elephantiasis, and malaria dropped dramatically. Often crops sprayed with DDT produced as much as double the normal yield.

However, Carson showed that the chemicals designed to kill harmful insects were building up in the soil and water. The chemicals were also building up in the bodies of animals. In addition, the chemicals destroyed useful insects as well as harmful ones.

By entering the food chain and eventually becoming concentrated in higher animals, pesticides were causing reproductive problems in birds of prey. It caused their eggshells to become too thin and fragile to develop normally. It took until 1973 for the government to ban the use of DDT in the United States.

Here is an example of how the entire food chain can be affected. Larger fish eat lots of smaller fish that have eaten lots of insects sprayed with pesticides. Then people eat the larger fish. During each step, the concentration of chemicals becomes greater.

Use the Internet or other reference sources to answer the following questions.

1. List some useful insects. _____

   _____

2. If there were no insects, would that be so bad? Why or why not? _____

   _____

   _____

3. Why did people think DDT was good at first? _____

   _____

   _____

4. What did Rachel Carson prove about the use of pesticides that was harmful? _____

   _____

   _____

5. If a small fish eats lots of insects that have been sprayed with a pesticide, what do you think happens?

   _____

   _____

Name: _____ Date: _____

ZIP into 1963

- The Post Office introduced ZIP codes in 1963.

- The first woman astronaut to travel in space was Valentina Tereshkova, a Russian, whose 49 orbits of Earth lasted three days. It wasn't until 1983 that Sally Ride became the first American woman to take part in an orbital mission.

- Federal legislation required "equal pay for equal work" for women.

- Douglas Engelbart received a patent for the computer mouse.

- The Emergency Broadcast System began periodic air tests.

- Sony™ offered an open-reel home videotape recorder for $995.

In 1963, the Post Office raised the cost of sending a one-ounce letter from four to five cents.

USA

- Polaroid™ instant film became available in color.

- Baseball great Willie Mays became the highest paid player when he signed with the San Francisco Giants for $100,000 a year.

- The first Boeing 727 took off. Nearly 2,000 of these aircraft were built before production stopped in 1984 to build bigger, better planes.

- The Supreme Court ruled that reading from the Bible in public schools was unconstitutional.

- Americans watched the first live televised murder when Jack Ruby shot Lee Harvey Oswald.

Use the Internet or other reference sources to answer the following questions.

1. What does ZIP stand for? _____

2. Why do you think it took so much longer for the United States to send a woman into space?

   _____

   _____

   _____

3. What is your opinion of the Supreme Court ruling regarding the Bible?

   _____

   _____

   _____

4. Who was Lee Harvey Oswald? _____

   _____

Name: _____ Date: _____

Dr. Martin Luther King, Jr.

Dr. Martin Luther King, Jr., had begun working against the segregation of Blacks in hotels, transportation, and housing in the 1950s. In 1963, more than 200,000 peaceful demonstrators joined King and other leaders for a march on Washington, D.C., to support the passage of civil rights laws.

As a result, Congress passed the Civil Rights Act of 1964, which prohibited segregation in public accommodations, education, and employment. For his work, King received the Nobel Peace Prize in 1964.

In 1968, while in Memphis, Tennessee, to support workers on strike, Martin Luther King, Jr., was shot and killed by James Earl Ray, an escaped White convict.

1. Use a dictionary. Define *segregation*.

   _____

   _____

2. Use a dictionary. Define *civil rights*.

   _____

   _____

Read the excerpt from Martin Luther King, Jr.'s "I Have a Dream" speech on the next page before completing the next section.

3. Write a short speech on your own paper about your dreams of freedom for yourself, your family, your community, or for America as a whole. Use Dr. King's speech as a model. Include convincing words that might influence others to feel the same way as you do about the future. Include ideas of what you can do to help make this dream come true. Make some notes below.

   _____

   _____

   _____

   _____

   _____

   _____

"I Have a Dream"

This is part of a speech delivered on the steps of the Lincoln Memorial by Dr. Martin Luther King, Jr., in Washington, D.C., on August 28, 1963.

"I say to you today, my friends, that in spite of the difficulties and frustrations of the moment, I still have a dream. It is a dream deeply rooted in the American dream.

I have a dream that one day this nation will rise up and live out the true meaning of its creed: 'We hold these truths to be self-evident: that all men are created equal.'

I have a dream that one day on the red hills of Georgia the sons of former slaves and the sons of former slaveowners will be able to sit down together at a table of brotherhood.

I have a dream that one day even the state of Mississippi ... will be transformed into an oasis of freedom and justice.

I have a dream that my four children will one day live in a nation where they will not be judged by the color of their skin but by the content of their character.

I have a dream today. I have a dream that one day ... little black boys and black girls will be able to join hands with little white boys and white girls and walk together as sisters and brothers.

[One day] ... we will be able to work together, to pray together, to struggle together, to go to jail together, to stand up for freedom together, knowing that we will be free one day.

This will be the day when all of God's children will be able to sing with a new meaning, 'My country, 'tis of thee, sweet land of liberty, of thee I sing. Land where my fathers died, land of the pilgrim's pride, from every mountainside, let freedom ring.'

And if America is to be a great nation, this must become true. So let freedom ring from the prodigious hilltops of New Hampshire! ... from the mighty mountains of New York! ... from the heightening Alleghenies of Pennsylvania! ... from the snowcapped Rockies of Colorado! ... from the curvaceous peaks of California! ... from Stone Mountain of Georgia! ...from Lookout Mountain of Tennessee! ... from every hill and every molehill of Mississippi. From every mountainside, let freedom ring.

When we let freedom ring, when we let it ring from every village and every hamlet, from every state and every city, we will be able to speed up that day when all of God's children ... will be able to join hands and sing, 'Free at last! Free at last! Thank God Almighty, we are free at last!'"

Name: _____ Date: _____

The Assassination of the President

Shots rang out as President Kennedy and his wife rode in a motorcade in Dallas, Texas, on Friday, November 22, 1963. The presidential limousine raced to the hospital, but the president was dead.

Most people who were alive in 1963 remember where they were and what they were doing when they heard the news that President Kennedy had died.

Lee Harvey Oswald, the man accused of shooting Kennedy, was never brought to trial. While police were moving him to a different jail, he was shot and killed by Jack Ruby.

Oswald's murder left many unanswered questions about the assassination. People wanted to know why he shot Kennedy and whether he acted on his own or was part of a conspiracy. Were Southern racists, Cubans, or the Central Intelligence Agency (CIA) to blame? Some rumors even accused Lyndon B. Johnson of planning the murder so he could become president.

Ninety minutes after the president died, Vice President Lyndon B. Johnson was sworn in as the 36th president. His oath of office was given aboard the presidential plane at an airport in Dallas.

President Johnson appointed the Warren Commission to investigate the assassination. The Warren Commission concluded that Oswald had acted alone and was not part of a conspiracy, but many felt their report had raised more questions than it had answered.

1. Ask two people you know who were born before 1963 if they remember where they were and what they were doing when they heard that John F. Kennedy had been shot. Write their responses below.

   a. _____

   _____

   b. _____

   _____

2. Why do you think many people still remember that event so clearly? _____

   _____

   _____

3. Why do you think Johnson was sworn into office so quickly? _____

   _____

   _____

Name: _____   Date: _____

What Happened in 1964?

- The Surgeon General released a report stating that smoking cigarettes was a definite health hazard. The warning, "Cigarette smoking may be hazardous to your health," first appeared on packs of cigarettes in this year.

- The Olympic Games in Tokyo were telecast live by satellite.

- Sidney Poitier became the first Black actor to receive an Oscar in a major category when he won an Academy Award for Best Actor for the film, *Lilies of the Field.*

- Japan introduced the videotape recorder for home use.

- *Mariner IV* sent television images from Mars.

- Martin Luther King, Jr., won the Nobel Peace Prize.

- Picturephones were tested between Disneyland and the New York World's Fair.

- Transpacific submarine telephone cable service began.

> C: > IBM's OS/360 became the first mass-produced computer operating system.
>
> C: > The PDP-8 minicomputer was the first to use integrated circuit technology.

- "Beatlemania" began in the United States with the arrival of the British rock group known as The Beatles. The "Fab Four" were featured on the popular "Ed Sullivan Show" and sold out at Carnegie Hall.

Use the Internet and other reference sources to answer the following questions.

1. Since they were invented so long ago, why do you think people do not have picturephones? Would you like to have one? Answer on your own paper.

2. Use a dictionary. Define *transpacific*. _____

_____

3. What were the names of the "Fab Four"?

_____

_____

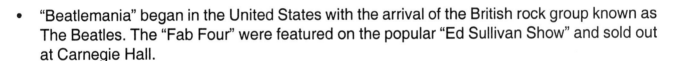

Ford Mustangs became available for the first time. Cost: $2,368. The average cost for a gallon of gas? 30 cents!

_____

_____

13

Name: _____ Date: _____

President Lyndon B. Johnson

In the 1964 presidential campaign, Johnson laid out a plan to create a "Great Society" for all Americans. He pledged to begin a "War on poverty, to provide greater educational opportunities for all American children, to offer medical care to the elderly, to conserve our water and air and natural resources, and to tackle the country's long-standing housing shortage."

Johnson told Congress: "We have talked long enough in this country about equal rights. We have talked for one hundred years or more. It is time now to write the next chapter and to write it in the books of law."

To achieve this goal, three important civil rights laws were passed. However, those who fought for civil rights were disappointed to discover that although the laws guaranteed equality, changing people's attitudes did not occur overnight.

When Lyndon B. Johnson became president in 1963, he promised to continue Kennedy's plans, including the passage of a civil rights bill and a tax reduction bill.

Johnson introduced programs like Head Start, Job Corps, Medicare, Neighborhood Youth Corps, and VISTA (Volunteers in Service to America). Johnson also provided federal aid programs to depressed Appalachia and started community action programs throughout America. Many people, particularly the middle class, criticized Johnson because these programs were costly to maintain, and they did not directly benefit from them.

In spite of the many domestic gains achieved while Johnson was president, the war in Southeast Asia overshadowed his term as president and caused a critical division of American opinion.

Anti-war protests, peace rallies, and demonstrations against U.S. involvement spread across the nation.

Although he would have been eligible to run for another term, Johnson decided not to run for reelection in 1968.

Answer the following questions.

1. How would you have answered critics if you had been President Johnson? _____

    _____

    _____

2. Do you think Johnson helped America become a "Great Society"? _____

    Why or why not? _____

    _____

14

Name: _____ Date: _____

Civil Rights Laws Passed

Three major pieces of civil rights legislation were passed while Lyndon B. Johnson was president.

The **Civil Rights Act of 1964** prohibited racial discrimination on the job, in public places, in government-owned facilities, unions, public schools, and federally funded programs. Approved on July 2, 1964, it was the most sweeping civil rights legislation passed up to that time.

Johnson knew that more laws were needed to give Blacks equal rights in other areas. Speaking to Congress, Johnson stated "... all of us must ... overcome the crippling legacy of bigotry and injustice. And ... we ... shall ... overcome."

Johnson convinced Congress to pass the **Voting Rights Act of 1965**, which eliminated literacy tests and poll taxes as conditions for voting.

The assassination of Martin Luther King, Jr., on April 4, 1968, touched off riots in Washington, D.C., and 125 other American cities. Congress reacted by passing the **Civil Rights Act of 1968**, which made it illegal to discriminate in the sale or rental of housing. The bill also made it a federal crime to interfere with voting, work, schooling, jury duty, or participation in federally assisted programs.

Use the Internet and other reference sources to answer the following questions.

1. Use a dictionary. Define *bigotry.* _____

_____

2. How does bigotry "cripple" a society? _____

_____

3. Use a dictionary. Define *literacy.* _____

_____

4. What is a poll tax? _____

_____

_____

5. Of the three civil rights bills described above, which do you think was the most important? Give reasons for your answer.

_____

_____

_____

_____

_____

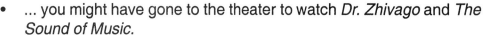

If You Were Alive in '65

If you were alive in 1965 ...

- ... you may have had milk delivered: 25 percent of all milk sold in 1965 was delivered to homes.

- ... you could have bought a 1966 model Ford that featured an 8-track tape player.

- ... you could have visited the "eighth wonder of the world"—the Houston Astrodome, which was the first roofed stadium.

- ... you could have bought Kodak™ Super 8 film for making your own home movies.

- ... you could have watched "A Charlie Brown Christmas" the first time it was shown on television.

- ... you could have seen several other TV shows for the first time this year, like "Green Acres," "The Dean Martin Show," "Hogan's Heroes," "The Smothers Brothers Show," and "I Dream of Jeannie."

- ... you could have bought one of the new cartridge audio tapes that went on sale this year.

- ... you could have been among the first to try a new product: Gatorade™.

- ... you could have listened to the Rolling Stones as they hit number one on the music charts for the first time with their song, "(I Can't Get No) Satisfaction."

- ... you could have met the Red Baron when he first appeared in the comic strip "Peanuts."

- ... you might have gone to the theater to watch *Dr. Zhivago* and *The Sound of Music*.

- ... If you were male, you could have been drafted. President Johnson increased the number of men drafted from 17,000 to 35,000 a month.

Talk to a friend or relative who remembers events from 1965. Ask that person to tell you about his or her memories from the mid-sixties. Share the remembrances with the class.

United States Involved in a No-Win War

Like Presidents Eisenhower and Kennedy, Johnson continued to provide American soldiers to help the South Vietnamese fight communist troops. As the war escalated, Johnson ordered bombing attacks against North Vietnam and committed more and more soldiers to the cause.

In spite of increasing expenditures of money, soldiers, and supplies, it became a no-win situation. Each week, the Department of Defense issued the latest "body counts"—U.S. soldiers killed. As the war dragged on, anti-war protests increased.

In May 1967, American planes bombed Hanoi, the capital of North Vietnam. U.S. casualties for one week rose to 3,000.

Although Johnson and U.S. military officials claimed that the United States was winning the war, the invasion of the North Vietnamese Army into South Vietnam in 1968 told another story. Even though Johnson halted the bombing raids and attempted peace negotiations, the war dragged on.

When Nixon took over as president in 1969, he attempted to find an "honorable" solution that would allow South Vietnam to become a free country. He increased assistance in training South Vietnamese soldiers and then extended bombing raids into Cambodia.

When he ordered the invasion of Cambodia to clear out North Vietnamese supply bases, antiwar protests increased. Peace talks bogged down, and U.S. involvement continued until January 1973 when a cease-fire agreement was eventually signed.

Although Nixon finally withdrew American troops, the war between North and South Vietnam continued until April 1975 when South Vietnam surrendered.

Answer the following questions on your own paper.

1. Do you think the United States has the right or obligation to help other countries fight wars? Why or why not?
2. Do you think the public has the right to protest against government actions if they believe the actions are wrong? Why or why not?
3. Some people feel it is the duty of all citizens to support their government's decisions, even if they do not agree. What is your opinion?

Name: _____ Date: _____

"Beam Me Up, Scotty"

- "Star Trek" premiered on TV in 1966. Although it was at the bottom of the ratings after its first season and only lasted three seasons, it went on to become the most popular science fiction show in television history. However, this only happened after the series had been canceled and brought back in reruns.

    Several movies with the original cast became popular as well as other series based on the original concept, such as: "Star Trek: The Next Generation," "Deep Space Nine," "Voyager," and "Enterprise."

- Hollywood adopted an age-based rating system in 1966: G, PG, R, X.

- One of the runners in the 1966 Boston Marathon hid in the bushes near the starting line. Wearing a hooded sweatshirt, the runner joined the others when the starting gun sounded. When the runner became too warm and removed the hood, the crowd discovered the runner was a woman! At that time, women were not allowed to enter the race.

    Running with 415 men, Roberta Bingay was the 124th person to cross the finish line in a time of 3 hours, 21 minutes. The rules were not changed, however, until six years later when women were finally included.

- Nearly 400,000 U.S. troops were in Southeast Asia by the end of 1966.

- If you've watched any police shows, you probably know about a famous decision made by the Supreme Court in 1966. The *Miranda Decision* gave individuals the right to remain silent because "... anything you say, can and will be used against you in a court of law."

    The court ruled that the Fifth Amendment "required warnings before valid statements could be taken by police." If police do not notify suspects of their Miranda Rights to remain silent and have an attorney present, anything said will not be admitted in court.

Use the Internet and other reference sources to answer the following questions.

1. Who played the lead roles of Captain Kirk and Mr. Spock on "Star Trek"?

   _____

2. What do you think of the Supreme Court decision regarding Miranda Rights and the Fifth Amendment?

   _____

   _____

   _____

3. A new organization, NOW, formed in 1966. What does NOW stand for?

   _____

Name: _____ Date: _____

Tune In, Turn On, Drop Out

Young Americans became very involved in the protest movements of the sixties. They spoke out against the war in Vietnam and pollution. They supported civil rights and individual freedom. They endorsed new values and a new lifestyle, rebelling against an "impersonal society."

The hippie movement involved a minority of people who were mostly young and from middle-class families. They rejected traditional American culture with its emphasis on materialism (possessions) and decided to "drop out" of society. Timothy Leary, a Harvard professor who was fired for supplying LSD (a hallucinogenic drug) to his students, became a major leader of the hippie counter-culture centered in the Haight-Ashbury section of San Francisco. (LSD was legal in California until 1966.)

The hippie lifestyle often centered on communal living. Hippies promoted peace, love, sharing, mutual respect, and brotherhood. They believed in freedom to do whatever they wanted, as long as it did not hurt someone else. They sought inner peace through drugs (particularly LSD and marijuana), meditation, religion, and self-analysis, which led to an interest in astrology and Eastern religions and philosophies.

The men grew beards and let their hair grow long. Their music of choice became hard rock. At concerts, fans and performers were often high on drugs. Hippies affected fashions, politics, music, poetry, movies, and the publication of underground magazines.

The term "generation gap" was used to describe the differences in opinions and attitudes between young people and their parents. Hippies paved the way for the do-your-own-thing mood that became an American symbol.

1. From what you've read, what do you think was good about the hippie movement?

   _____

   _____

   _____

2. From what you've read, what do you think was wrong with the hippie movement?

   _____

   _____

   _____

   _____

Name: _____ Date: _____

Sixties Scavenger Hunt

To complete this scavenger hunt, use the Internet and other reference sources to find the answers.

1. One of the most popular dances of the '60s began when 19-year-old Chubby Checker's song, "Let's Twist," rose to the top of the charts in 1961. What was Chubby Checker's real name? _____

2. Muhammad Ali defeated Sonny Liston in 1964 to become the heavyweight boxing champion. What was the champ's name before he changed it to Muhammad Ali?

   _____

3. The first "Peanuts" TV special, "A Charlie Brown Christmas" aired in 1965. Who created Charlie Brown and his friends? _____

4. CRASH! POW! KA-POW! The dynamic duo of Batman and Robin came to television in 1966. Who played Batman and Robin in the series "Batman"?

   _____

5. Besides the twist, young people did other dances with colorful names during the '60s. Which of these were not the names of dances: hot potato; monster mash; mashed potato; the squash; the frug; the jerk; the stroll; the limbo; the pony; the wiggle wobble?

   _____

6. When John F. Kennedy was president, his daughter Caroline often rode her pet pony on the White House lawn. What was the name of Caroline's pony? _____

7. Ronald McDonald made his debut as a representative of the McDonald hamburger chain in Washington, D.C., in 1962. Who was the first Ronald McDonald?

   _____

8. In 1963, the New York Titans of the American Football League changed their name. What team did they become? _____

9. A musical group known as the Blue Velvets decided to change its name in 1968. The group soon climbed to stardom as a national pop music favorite. What was the group's new name? _____

10. Postage rates increased a penny in 1968. What was the new rate for a one-ounce letter?

   _____

What Happened in 1967?

- Snoopy and Charlie Brown of the comic strip "Peanuts" were featured on the cover of *LIFE* magazine.

- Computer light pens became available.

- The United States began Daylight Saving Time.

- Newspapers introduced computers into their operations.

- ABC joined CBS and NBC in presenting 30-minute television newscasts.

- Thurgood Marshall became the first Black Supreme Court Justice.

- A report by the Southern Education Reporting Service stated that 16 percent of Black students in 11 southern states were attending desegregated schools in 1967.

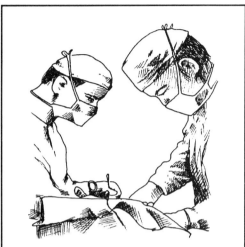

Dr. Christiaan Barnard performed the first successful heart transplant. The patient, Louis Washkansky, lived for 18 days with the new heart.

- New magazines in this year included *Rolling Stone* and *New York*.

- State laws forbidding interracial marriages were ruled unconstitutional by the Supreme Court.

- *Mariner 5* was launched toward Venus.

- Muhammad Ali refused induction into the U.S. Army. As a result, his world heavyweight crown was later taken away. He was fined $10,000 and sentenced to five years in prison. He claimed his actions were based on religious grounds.

Write your answers on your own paper.

1. Do you think Muhammed Ali's punishment was fair? Why or why not?

2. Of the events listed on this page and the next page, which surprise you the most? Why?

Jim Ryun set a new world record for the mile: 3 minutes, 51.1 seconds.

Name: _____ Date: _____

Then and Now

Read the statements about 1967. Add a statement about how things are the same or different today.

1. **Then:** For the first time, sales of color TV sets outnumbered sales of black-and-white sets.

   Now: _____

   _____

   _____

2. **Then:** In 1967, Amana™ introduced the first compact microwave oven for home use with a price tag of $495.

   Now: _____

   _____

   _____

3. **Then:** The Green Bay Packers defeated the Kansas City Chiefs in Super Bowl I held in Los Angeles. The Most Valuable Player was quarterback Bart Starr. Fans paid $10 for tickets.

   Now: _____

   _____

   _____

4. **Then:** IBM introduced the floppy disk.

   Now: _____

   _____

   _____

5. **Then:** Cordless telephones first entered the phone system.

   Now: _____

   _____

   _____

6. **Then:** Pre-recorded movies on videotape were sold for use with home video players.

   Now: _____

   _____

   _____

Name: _____ Date: _____

1968: A Turbulent Year

- The assassination of Martin Luther King, Jr., in Memphis by James Earl Ray led to an increase in race riots in parts of the United States.

- Magnetic-strip credit cards became available.

- Intelsat completed the global communications satellite loop.

- Robert Kennedy, brother of John Kennedy, won the nomination for president in the California primary on June 5. That same evening, he was shot and killed in Los Angeles.

- Intel marketed a one-KB RAM microchip.

- Shirley Chisholm became the first Black woman elected to Congress.

- Violence erupted during the Democratic presidential convention between antiwar demonstrators and the Chicago police.

- The cost of mailing a letter increased to six cents.

- The price of Hershey™ chocolate bars doubled—to 10 cents each.

Use the Internet and other reference sources to answer the following questions.

A. What does KB mean? _____

B. How many KB equals one megabyte (MB)? _____

C. How many MB equals one gigabyte (GB)? _____

D. Check an ad for a new computer online or in a newspaper. How much memory does the computer have? _____

The younger generation coined new phrases in the sixties. Ask older friends or relatives to help you match the words and phrases with their meanings.

_____ 1. hung up   A. to lose touch with reality or to lose control

_____ 2. hairy   B. someone very involved with a certain thing, such as music or food

_____ 3. heavy   C. terrific

_____ 4. freak out   D. frightening

_____ 5. freak   E. unable to make a decision

_____ 6. groovy   F. profound

Name: _____   Date: _____

Environmental Awareness

As the decade wore on, the growth of industry and demands for bigger cars and more goods created more polluted air, soil, and water. Pollution killed fish, plants, birds, and other wildlife.

Thanks to Rachel Carson, public awareness about the effects of DDT and pesticides on wildlife and the environment led to action. Congress passed the Wilderness Act in 1964 to set aside "an area where earth and its community of life are untrammeled by man."

Lyndon B. Johnson stated in 1965: "There is no excuse for a river flowing red with blood from slaughterhouses ... for paper mills pouring tons of sulfuric acid into the lakes and streams ... for chemical companies and refineries using our major rivers as pipelines for toxic wastes ... for communities to use the people's rivers as a dump for raw sewage."

Congress passed the first antipollution bill in October 1965, authorizing the Secretary of Health, Education, and Welfare to establish emission standards for automobiles and ban the sale of any cars not meeting those standards.

The Air Quality Act of 1967 took another big step toward cleaning up and protecting the environment. More than $428 million was set aside for a three-year fight against air pollution.

"Either we stop poisoning our air or we become a nation of gas masks, groping our way through the dying cities and a wilderness of ghost towns."

By the late sixties, attempts to reverse the effects of pollution were in full swing. Recycling centers opened. Several grassroots organizations were founded, including the Environmental Defense Fund (1967), Friends of the Environment (1968), and Greenpeace (1970).

1. Describe three ways you and your family help preserve the environment.

_____

_____

_____

_____

_____

_____

_____

_____

2. Use reference sources to learn more about: (A) a national environmental organization or (B) another federal environmental protection law passed in the 1960s or 1970s. On your own paper, write a summary of what you learned.

Name: _____ Date: _____

In the News in 1969

The purpose of a headline is to catch the readers' attention. Use six words or less to write a newspaper headline for each item.

1. _____

   The *Saturday Evening Post* magazine stopped publication. Television was blamed for the magazine's failure.

2. _____

   The FCC banned broadcast advertising of tobacco in the United States.

3. _____

   In spite of bad weather and traffic jams, between 300,000 and 400,000 people showed up at a 600-acre farm in New York to attend Woodstock, a three-day, nonstop outdoor rock concert.

4. _____

   The draft lottery began. Men were drafted into the military if their numbers came up.

5. _____

   Yankee Stadium in New York City was sold out as Mickey Mantle formally retired from baseball.

6. _____

   Leonard Tose paid $16,155,000 to buy the NFL team, the Philadelphia Eagles. It was the largest price paid to that date for a pro-football franchise.

7. _____

   Dr. Denton Cooley performed the first artificial heart transplant.

8. _____

   To celebrate his 70th birthday, Duke Ellington was presented with the Medal of Freedom, the U.S. government's highest civilian honor.

9. _____

   A federal truth-in-lending law went into effect requiring that charges for credit and loans be made clear to borrowers.

10. _____

   The Boeing 747 made its first public flight. It cost $21,400,000 to build one plane.

Name: _____ Date: _____

President Nixon's First Term

In the 1952 presidential election, Richard Nixon was elected vice president. After two terms, Nixon was chosen as the Republican candidate for president, but he lost to John F. Kennedy in the 1960 election. When he also lost the election in 1962 for governor of California, it appeared that his political career might be over. Nixon returned to his legal career, setting up practice in New York.

When Lyndon Johnson decided not to run for reelection in 1968, Richard M. Nixon was nominated by the Republicans. He became president in January 1969.

Nixon inherited a very unpopular war in Southeast Asia. Americans watched the horrors of war on the nightly news. Weekly announcements listed the number killed, wounded, or missing in action. Although Nixon attempted peace talks several times, U.S. involvement in the war continued until a cease-fire agreement in 1973 when American troops were finally withdrawn.

During Nixon's first term as president, Congress passed strong anti-crime laws and cut taxes. Progress was made in civil rights and equal opportunities for women. Nixon worked for reforms in welfare, health care, and environmental programs.

The United States had cut off relations with China when the Communists took over in 1950. Nixon supported China's admission to the United Nations. He became the first president to visit both China and Russia. His efforts led to trade relations with China and to the first Strategic Arms Limitation Treaty with Russia.

In June 1971, the *New York Times* published what were called the Pentagon Papers given to them by a former Pentagon aide. The papers revealed that Nixon and the Pentagon had not told Congress the truth about how the Vietnam War was going and about U.S. involvement in it.

A series of "news leaks"—information given to the press without the knowledge or permission of the government—followed. To discover who was leaking information to the press, Nixon ordered wiretaps on many of the White House phones. He also had microphones hidden in several offices to record conversations he had with others.

1. Do you think Nixon was right or wrong to tap phones and record private conversations in an attempt to find the leak? Give specific reasons for your opinion.

_____

_____

_____

_____

Name: _____ Date: _____

To the Moon—and Back

Tragedy canceled the United States' plans to send astronauts to the moon in 1967. Three astronauts scheduled to make the first trip to the moon on *Apollo 1* were killed during a routine test when the oxygen in the capsule burst into flames. Those killed were Ed White, Gus Grissom, and Roger Chaffee.

Four days later, two astronauts died in another fire in a flight simulator. All manned flights were canceled for over a year.

Finally, in December 1968, *Apollo 8* carried three men into orbit around the moon and back to Earth.

Eventually, the stage was set for the next mission: landing men on the moon and returning them safely to Earth. After a four-day journey, three astronauts aboard *Apollo 11* reached their destination.

After orbiting the moon, Neil Armstrong and Edwin "Buzz" Aldrin landed the lunar module *Eagle* on the surface of the moon on July 20, 1969.

An estimated 600 million people watched as Neil Armstrong became the first person to walk on the moon's surface. Most who saw the event remember his first words: "That's one small step for man, one giant leap for mankind."

While on the moon, Armstrong and Aldrin set up a solar wind experiment, a seismometer to detect moonquakes, and a laser reflector, which allowed scientists to make very accurate measurements of the distance from Earth to the moon.

The astronauts brought back samples of rocks and soil from the moon. Before they left, they planted an American flag and erected a plaque attached to the landing craft's descent stage. On the plaque was a map of Earth, the signatures of Richard M. Nixon and the three astronauts, and these words:

HERE MEN FROM THE PLANET EARTH
FIRST SET FOOT UPON THE MOON
JULY 1969, A.D.
WE CAME IN PEACE FOR ALL MANKIND

1. Knowing the tragedies that had happened during the testing and training, how would you have felt if you were one of the people training to be an astronaut?

_____

2. Use the Internet and other reference sources. Who was the third astronaut on this mission with Armstrong and Aldrin? _____

3. What do you think Armstrong meant in his first words when walking on the moon?

_____

_____

Name: _____ Date: _____

Can You Tell Me How to Get to Sesame Street?

Television allowed millions of Americans to see a place never before visited by a human being when they watched the historical moon landing and first moon walk. In 1969, television also took Americans to another place no one had ever seen before—Sesame Street. Astronauts did not find little green space men on the moon, but children were delighted to find Sesame Street populated with colorful monsters, a talking frog, a huge, fuzzy, yellow bird, and other "muppet" characters created by Jim Henson.

Almost every child born in the United States since 1969 can easily identify Bert, Ernie, Big Bird, Oscar the Grouch, Cookie Monster, Kermit the Frog, the Count, and others. The Sesame Street gang became part of most children's early education as they sang the alphabet song with their muppet friends and counted with the Count.

Not only did Sesame Street give children a colorful, fun way to learn the letters of the alphabet, words, and numbers, but it also provided lessons in social skills such as cooperation, resolving differences peacefully, and getting along with others who may be very different.

1. Who was your favorite Sesame Street character when you were younger? Why?

   _____

   _____

   _____

   _____

2. Write a review of Sesame Street. Include your opinion and reasons why the show is good or not good for young children. Include at least one recommendation of how you think the show could be better.

   _____

   _____

   _____

   _____

   _____

   _____

   _____

   _____

Name: _____ Date: _____

Who's Who?

Women's Liberation was an important issue in the sixties and seventies, and many American women made breakthroughs in sports, medicine, politics, art, science, and other fields. Use the Internet and other reference sources if you need help matching the women below with their areas of fame. Some answers may be used more than once.

_____ 1. Peggy Fleming
_____ 2. Betty Friedan
_____ 3. Grace Murray Hopper
_____ 4. Rachel Carson
_____ 5. Billie Jean King
_____ 6. Shirley Chisholm
_____ 7. Barbara McClintock
_____ 8. Ella Fitzgerald
_____ 9. Beverly Cleary
_____ 10. Aretha Franklin
_____ 11. Edith Spurlock Sampson
_____ 12. Wilma Rudolph
_____ 13. Fannie Lou Hammer
_____ 14. Maria Tallchief
_____ 15. Bella Abzug
_____ 16. Shirley Temple Black
_____ 17. Georgia O'Keeffe
_____ 18. Barbara Harris
_____ 19. Mary Martin
_____ 20. Barbara Jordan
_____ 21. Anna Mae Aquash
_____ 22. Coretta Scott King

A. Actress
B. Artist
C. Author
D. Civil Rights activist
E. Clergywoman
F. Computer pioneer
G. Dancer
H. Diplomat
I. Judge
J. Member of Congress
K. Musician/Singer
L. Native American rights activist
M. Olympic medal winner
N. Tennis professional
O. Scientist
P. Women's lib advocate

Rachel Carson

Shirley Temple Black

Name: _____   Date: _____

Fashions in the Sixties

Fashions for men and women varied widely during the 1960s from high fashion to non-fashion. Many women imitated the clothing, hats, and hairstyles worn by the "First Lady of Fashion," Jackie Kennedy. Other influences on fashion included The Beatles, movies and television shows, pop art, and the "space age." Men began wearing brighter colors and less formal suits. By the end of the decade, the non-fashion of the hippies had influenced clothing and hairstyles.

Match the pictures with their descriptions.

_____ 1. Bell-bottom jeans

_____ 2. Pillbox hat

_____ 3. Mini skirt

_____ 4. Maxi skirt

_____ 5. Mini A-line dress

_____ 6. Tie-dye

_____ 7. Paisley design

_____ 8. Caftan

_____ 9. Beatles jacket

_____ 10. Midi skirt

_____ 11. Pop-art style

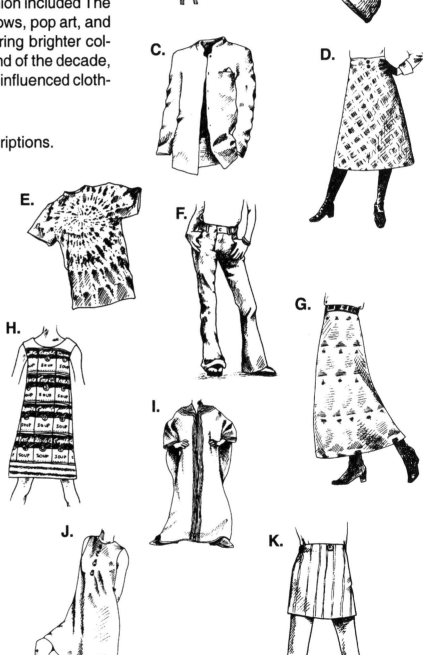

1. Which of the styles shown do you like best and why? Are some of these styles popular today? Write about it on your own paper.

Name: _____ Date: _____

Jeopardy!

Category: The sixties.

Please be sure your answers are in the form of a question. The first one has been done for you.

1. One of television's best-known game shows aired on NBC for the first time in 1964 with host Art Fleming.

    Question: What was *Jeopardy!*?

2. Elected in 1960, he became the first Catholic president and the youngest man elected president.

    Question: _____?

3. The event marked "one small step for man, one giant leap for mankind."

    Question: _____?

4. This civil rights leader gave his "I Have a Dream" speech in 1963.

    Question: _____?

5. From England, the group known as the "Fab Four" became an instant success in the United States.

    Question: _____?

6. He fought a "war on poverty" and laid plans for a "Great Society."

    Question: _____?

7. This marine biologist warned people about the dangers of pesticides, particularly DDT.

    Question: _____?

8. Children who visited here made new friends and found a fun way to learn letters, words, numbers, and social skills.

    Question: _____?

9. This science fiction television series starring Captain Kirk and Mr. Spock became more popular after it was canceled and reruns began.

    Question: _____?

10. A decision made by the Supreme Court in 1966 gave people the right to remain silent because " ... anything you say, can and will be used against you in a court of law."

    Question: _____?

Name: _____ Date: _____

The 1970s

The 1970s were a decade of contrasts and tensions. At the beginning of the '70s, the United States was still deeply involved in the unpopular war in Southeast Asia.

The resignation of Vice President Agnew, the Watergate scandal, and the eventual resignation of President Nixon led many people to distrust government and political leaders.

Encouraged by progress made by Black Americans in the '60s, other groups, including Hispanic Americans and Native Americans, began their own struggles for equal rights. The Women's Rights Movement also gained momentum.

A major change in men's fashions took place in the mid-seventies with the introduction of polyester "leisure suits," which were available in bright shades of purple, rose, orange, and lime green. Both men and women began wearing high platform shoes and bell-bottom jeans.

Among the top movies of the decade were *Jaws* (1975), *Rocky* (1976), *Star Wars* (1977), *Close Encounters of the Third Kind* (1977), and *Grease* (1978).

Unlike 1960 where three of the five top TV shows that year were Westerns, only *Gunsmoke* remained in the top five by 1970. The other leading shows in 1970 were "The Flip Wilson Show"; "Marcus Welby, M.D."; "All in the Family"; and "Sanford and Son." By 1972, no Westerns remained in the top five.

Many of the television shows that became popular in the seventies reflected nostalgia for earlier, simpler times like "Happy Days," "Laverne and Shirley," "Little House on the Prairie," and "The Waltons."

Disco (short for "discothèque") became the biggest new trend in music. By 1978, there were approximately 20,000 disco clubs in the country where millions danced to steady pulsing beats while strobe lights flashed.

One of the biggest changes of the decade came in electronics with the development of the silicon chip. Computers evolved from the huge, room-sized, expensive models of the 1960s to the first practical personal computers. The "computer age" had begun.

1. Which of the above television shows have you seen as reruns? _____

_____

_____

2. Of the ones you've seen, which do you like best? Why? _____

_____

_____

_____

Name: _____ Date: _____

What Happened in 1970?

- For the first time, women were promoted to the rank of general in the U.S. Army.

- The Postal Reform Bill made the U.S. Postal Service an independent organization.

- OSHA became a new government agency.

- Nixon announced the invasion of Cambodia by American troops.

- National Guardsmen were called out to control student demonstrations at Kent State University. Students were protesting the dropping of bombs on Cambodia. Angered by the presence of National Guardsmen, students began yelling and throwing stones. The troops fired, killing four students and wounding eight others.

- The Associated Press began sending news by computer.

- The computer floppy disk became an instant success. These were the 5 1/4-inch disks. (The 3 1/2-inch disks weren't available until 1984.)

- The first National Earth Day was celebrated on April 22, 1970.

- A new government organization, the EPA, was formed to establish standards to prevent and control pollution, toxic waste, and radioactive waste.

- Corning Glass Works invented an optical fiber clear enough to carry light pulses.

- The 1970 census showed the population of the United States at 203,302,031.

Use the Internet and other reference sources to answer the following questions.

1. What does OSHA stand for? _____

    _____

2. If you had been a student at Kent State University in 1970, what do you think your reaction would have been to the actions of the National Guardsmen?

    _____

    _____

    _____

3. What does EPA stand for? _____

Name: _____ Date: _____

Pop Goes the Art World

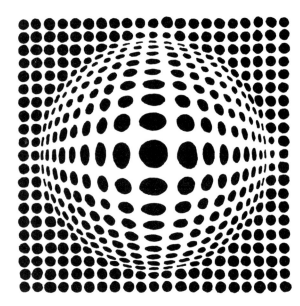

The abstract style of art made popular by Jackson Pollock and other artists in the 1950s gave way in the '60s to a new form called Op Art. Artists rejected the spontaneous approach and created carefully planned, brightly-colored, realistic designs often comprised of geometric figures, like circles and squares.

Op Art made use of optical illusions and other visual effects that often appeared to give the impression of an image forming and reforming. American artists like **Kenneth Noland**, **Frank Stella**, and **Ad Reinhardt** made Op Art popular for a brief time.

Op Art led to **Pop Art** in which artists used images from everyday life, such as numbers, letters, road signs, cartoons, posters, product packages, popular music, and science fiction, as themes for their paintings.

Andy Warhol used a silk-screening technique that allowed him to repeat an image over and over in the same painting. He became famous for his images of Campbell's™ Soup cans, boxes of Kellogg's™ Corn Flakes, and Marilyn Monroe.

A trend began for creating several paintings depicting a similar theme. **Jasper Johns** painted a series of American flags and another of bull's-eye targets. **Robert Indiana**'s paintings depicted large numbers and letters inside squares and circles. **Roy Lichtenstein** enlarged individual frames from comic strips painted on large canvases. Pop Art also influenced sculptors like **Claes Oldenburg** and **George Segal**.

Using the Internet and other reference sources, look carefully at several paintings done by one of the artists listed above during the sixties or seventies. Then choose one of these options:

A.   Write your opinion of that artist's work on your own paper,

OR

B.   Do a drawing in color in the Op Art or Pop Art style.

Name: _____ Date: _____

In the News in 1971

- Intel built the 4004 microprocessor, "a computer on a chip." The microprocessor chip has become the foundation of all computers and nearly everything else electronic.

- A new programming language, Pascal, was introduced.

- Project Gutenberg began to enter great documents and literature online.

- Cigarette ads were banned on television.

- Waterbeds became a national fad.

- The Magic Kingdom at Disney World opened in Orlando, Florida.

- The use of bussing to end segregation in public schools was ruled constitutional by the Supreme Court.

- The Washington Senators moved to Texas and were renamed the Texas Rangers.

- Direct-dial between New York and London became available; previously, operators had had to connect long-distance calls.

- Bobby Fischer became the first person from the United States to win a world championship in his field.

- The Wang 1200 was the first word processor.

- Beatle George Harrison organized the first benefit concert for Bangladesh, which became the model for many more benefit concerts, especially in the '80s.

Use the Internet and other reference sources to answer the following questions.

1. Do you think the government has the right to ban ads for any legal product? Why or why not?

_____

_____

_____

_____

2. Who is your all-time favorite Disney character? _____

3. What sport did the Senators play? _____

4. What was Bobby Fischer's field? _____

5. What is Bangladesh? _____

_____

Name: _____   Date: _____

Headline News

Write a headline in six words or less for each 1971 news item.

1. _____

   An earthquake in California killed 65 people and caused $500,000,000 in damages.

2. _____

   David Scott, James Irwin, and Alfred Worden made the fourth successful moon landing by U.S. astronauts. They collected rock samples estimated to be about four billion years old.

3. _____

   The cost to mail a one-ounce letter increased from six to eight cents.

4. _____

   NASA and the Soviets sent probes to Mars. On November 14, the NASA *Mariner 9* became the first spacecraft to orbit another planet. The Soviets' *Mars 2* and *Mars 3* arrived a month later and sent a probe down to the planet (which unfortunately didn't work for long).

5. _____

   The Kennedy Center for the Performing Arts opened in Washington, D.C.

6. _____

   The most important medical breakthrough since the X-ray, Computerized Axial Tomography (CAT) scanning, became available.

7. _____

   During a riot at Attica State Prison in Buffalo, New York, 1,200 inmates took 30 guards and other employees prisoner in an attempt for reforms. The incident ended in a bloodbath four days later with 28 inmates and 9 guards dead, all killed by police gunfire when they took the prison back.

8. _____

   The voting age was lowered from 21 to 18 when the Twenty-sixth Amendment to the Constitution was ratified.

What Was New in '72?

- **New magazine:** *Ms* magazine was first published.

- **New game:** Pong, the first home video game, went on sale.

- **New rules:** Due to hijackings, the screening of passengers and luggage became mandatory on all domestic and foreign flights by American planes.

- **New agents:** Joanne Pierce and Susan Roley became the first female FBI agents.

- **New amendment:** Congress approved the Equal Rights Amendment (ERA) to provide equal rights between men and women, including equal pay for equal work. However, the amendment failed to be approved in the required three-fourths of states and was not added to the Constitution.

- **New telescope:** Copernicus was launched into orbit as an astronomical observatory designed to study the stars and the nature of the universe.

- **Travel news:** President Nixon become the first U.S. President to visit China and Russia. A 22-year ban on travel to China was lifted later in the year.

- **New record:** On November 14, the Dow Jones Average hit 1000 for the first time in history.

- **New museum:** The only museum devoted exclusively to jazz, the New York Jazz Museum, opened.

- **Religion news:** Sally J. Priesand was the first woman in the United States to become an ordained rabbi.

- **Computer news:** Public demonstrations of ARPANET began. This system for transferring data between university computers later developed into the Internet.

- **New Olympic record:** U.S. swimmer Mark Spitz set an Olympic record by winning seven gold medals in the summer games.

- **New park:** Alcatraz became a national park.

1. Of the "new" items listed, which do you think has had the most impact on your life? Why? Write your answer on your own paper.

Name: _____ Date: _____

What Was Watergate?

On June 17, 1972, police arrested five suspected burglars at the Democratic National Headquarters at the Watergate Building Complex in Washington, D.C. Searches of their rooms at the Watergate Hotel revealed telephone-tapping devices, tear-gas guns, cameras, walkie-talkies, burglary tools, and $4,500 in new one-hundred-dollar bills. (Later, investigators discovered that the money had come directly from President Richard Nixon's campaign funds.)

One of the burglars was John W. McCord, security chief for the Committee to Reelect the President (CREEP). The other four were Cuban-Americans. Investigators found that a month earlier the same five men had installed secret electronic listening devices to monitor Democratic campaign plans.

The Director of CREEP, John Mitchell, former U.S. Attorney General, publicly stated that "McCord and the other four men arrested in Democratic Headquarters ... were not operating either on our behalf or with our consent in the alleged bugging." He continued by saying, "There is no place in our campaign or in the electoral process for this type of activity, and we will not permit or condone it."

Continued investigations revealed that two other men had been inside the Watergate building at the time, but hadn't been caught. One was G. Gordon Liddy, a former FBI agent and legal financial advisor for CREEP. The other, E. Howard Hunt, was a former CIA agent and consultant paid by the White House.

On August 29, 1972, President Nixon stated: "I can state categorically that ... no one in this administration, presently employed, was involved in this very bizarre incident."

In September, a Washington grand jury charged the seven men with crimes related to the Watergate burglary, but they did not go on trial until January 1973.

In spite of everything that had already been made public, Richard Nixon was reelected as president in November 1972. He won every electoral vote except those from Massachusetts and the District of Columbia.

1. Why do you think so many people voted for Nixon, under the circumstances?

_____

_____

_____

_____

2. Would you have voted for him? Why or why not? _____

_____

_____

_____

_____

Name: _____ Date: _____

Prices Rose in 1973

- The Miami Dolphins became the first NFL team to have a perfect season. They won every game including Super Bowl VII. Tickets to the big game had increased 50 percent since Super Bowl I—they cost $15!

- OPEC increased the price of oil, beginning the gas crisis of the '70s. Oil went from $1.50 to $11.56 a barrel over the course of a few months in retaliation for U.S. support of Israel.

- Pepsi-Cola™ became the first American product licensed for sale in the Soviet Union.

- *People* magazine was first published.

- Spiro T. Agnew resigned as Vice President of the United States.

- The use of DDT was banned in the United States.

- The United States launched its first space station. *Skylab* had a workshop and living quarters where three teams of astronauts lived and worked for 172 days while orbiting Earth.

- Tennis pro Bobby Riggs bragged that no woman could beat him. Billie Jean King took the challenge and forced him to eat his words while 40 to 50 million television viewers watched.

- UPC barcodes were first introduced.

- The Sears Tower in Chicago opened. At 1,454 feet tall, it was the world's tallest building at that time.

- Congress passed the War Powers Act, which would prevent the president from committing U.S. forces abroad for more than 60 days without Congressional approval.

- The last U.S. combat ground forces were withdrawn from Vietnam.

Use the Internet and other reference sources to answer the following questions.

1. What do the letters OPEC stand for? _____

_____

2. Who became the new vice president when Spiro T. Agnew resigned?

_____

3. If you had the opportunity to live for a year on a space station, would you take it? Why or why not?

_____

_____

_____

4. What does UPC mean? _____

The Second Battle of Wounded Knee

In the late sixties, Native American activists founded the American Indian Movement (AIM) to promote cultural awareness, political self-determination, and protection of lands from further seizure by the government.

AIM organized several protests to draw attention to the poor conditions on Native American reservations. In 1972, about 500 members of AIM took control of the Bureau of Indian Affairs (BIA) in Washington, D.C., in a "Trail of Broken Treaties" protest against treaty violations. This resulted in some changes and a closer look at AIM's grievances.

On February 27, 1973, members of AIM seized and held the Pine Ridge Reservation in South Dakota. Federal law officials blockaded the reservation and arrested everyone who tried to bring supplies in during a 71-day standoff. Two Native Americans were killed, and several people on both sides were wounded.

This became known as the Second Battle of Wounded Knee because it was near the site of the 1890 battle where Native Americans were massacred in the last major clash between federal troops and Native Americans.

AIM wanted to stop the tribal government from giving nearly 80,000 acres of land to the federal government. AIM members also wanted free elections of tribal leaders, investigation into complaints against the BIA, and a review of all United States-Native American treaties.

The siege continued until May 8 when the federal government agreed to investigate the complaints. However, only one meeting took place with a White House representative. A second meeting was promised, but it never occurred.

Nevertheless, AIM succeeded in bringing national attention to Native American problems. Congress passed the Indian Self-Determination and Educational Assistance Act of 1975. This law and others helped Native Americans assume control over many federal programs under the BIA.

1. What does AIM stand for? _____

   _____

2. What does BIA stand for? _____

   _____

3. If you had been a member of AIM at that time, would you have been satisfied with the action taken by the government? Why or why not?

   _____

   _____

   _____

   _____

   _____

Name: _____ Date: _____

The President Resigns

Although President Nixon had won an overwhelming victory in the 1972 election, public confidence declined as investigators slowly revealed the truth about Watergate and the attempted cover-up.

Five of the seven men charged by the grand jury in the Watergate break-in pleaded guilty to burglary, conspiracy, and illegal wiretapping. All seven were convicted and sentenced to prison.

The Senate created a "select committee" to investigate the Watergate affair. They gathered evidence for several months before beginning public hearings in May 1973. James McCord, one of those convicted, claimed that White House officials had covered up their involvement in the scandal and pressured the defendants into pleading guilty. He also stated that several witnesses had lied under oath.

Nixon addressed the nation on April 30, 1973, admitting " ... there had been an effort to conceal the facts," and blaming his staff. He claimed no knowledge of events and also claimed complete innocence.

The televised hearings lasted most of the summer. John Mitchell admitted he had lied under oath and that the break-in had been approved by Committee to Reelect the President (CREEP) officials. Others claimed Mitchell had approved the wiretapping in advance.

Evidence related to other illegal activities also came to light. Nixon campaign workers had ruined the chances of several Democratic candidates by publishing lies about them. Contributions to Nixon's campaign had been accepted in exchange for promises of future favors. Unreported funds were used to finance Watergate and other types of fraud.

When the committee learned that Nixon had secretly been taping White House conversations since 1970, they requested the tapes. Under pressure, Nixon finally released some tapes, but some parts had been erased. For a time, Nixon refused to hand over 64 additional tapes. Before the contents of the tapes became public, the House Judiciary Committee voted to impeach Nixon. Rather than face an impeachment trial, Nixon resigned, effective August 9, 1974.

1. Considering what else had been made public by then, if you had heard Nixon's speech, do you think you would have believed him? Why or why not?

_____

_____

_____

2. Some who were involved were sentenced to prison, but the president was not tried or convicted of any crimes. Do you think Nixon should have been tried and sent to prison if found guilty? Why or why not?

_____

_____

_____

Name: _____ Date: _____

Meet Gerald R. Ford

True or False? Gerald R. Ford was the first man to become president without being elected either president or vice president.

True. When Vice President Spiro Agnew resigned, President Nixon nominated Ford to replace him. Both Houses of Congress voted to accept him. A year later when Nixon also resigned, Vice President Ford became president.

Before accepting him as vice president, Congress did a thorough background check on Ford and asked him many questions.

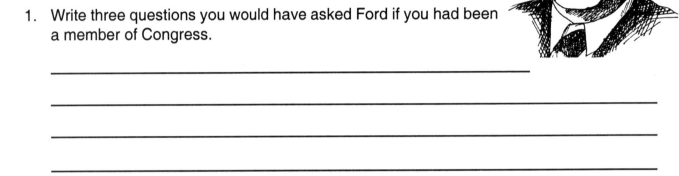

1. Write three questions you would have asked Ford if you had been a member of Congress.

_____

_____

_____

_____

Use the Internet or other reference sources to check out these statements about Gerald Ford. Circle "T" for true or "F" for false.

T   F   2.   When he was born, his parents named him Leslie.

T   F   3.   Ford grew up in Grand Rapids, Michigan.

T   F   4.   After college, Ford turned down offers to play professional football.

T   F   5.   Ford graduated from Harvard with a degree in microbiology.

T   F   6.   While in college, Ford worked with a modeling agency and appeared in magazine photos.

T   F   7.   Ford was elected to the U.S. Senate for six terms.

T   F   8.   While he was president, two attempts were made on Ford's life by women with guns. Both were convicted and sentenced to life in prison.

T   F   9.   Ford was a Democrat.

T   F   10. Ford was elected for a second term in 1976.

Name: _____ Date: _____

Ford Grants Pardons in 1974

- Four weeks after he became president, Gerald Ford granted Richard Nixon a full pardon for any crimes he might have committed while president. Many people were outraged by this action.

- Scientists announced that chlorofluorocarbons (CFCs) were causing damage to the ozone layer around Earth.

- The cost of a first-class stamp went from 8 cents to 10 cents.

- The *Wall Street Journal* successfully transmitted an edition by satellite.

- U.S. newspapers began replacing reporters' typewriters with computer terminals.

- The word "Internet" was first used.

- Minimum wage was raised to $2.30 an hour.

- Ford granted a limited amnesty to Vietnam War draft evaders and military deserters on the condition they perform public service for two years. Of the 106,000 men eligible, only 22,000 applied for amnesty.

1. What is your opinion of Ford's full pardon for Richard Nixon?

   _____

   _____

   _____

2. Use a dictionary. Define *amnesty*. _____

   _____

   Do you think the conditions of Ford's amnesty were fair for draft evaders and military deserters? Why or why not?

   _____

   _____

   _____

3. Why do you think so few men applied for amnesty?

   _____

   _____

   _____

Name: _____ Date: _____

What Happened in 1975?

- There were two attempts to assassinate President Ford.

- Philips™ demonstrated an optical videodisc system.

- BASIC became the first programming language for the personal computer.

- Steven Spielberg's *Jaws* became the first film to earn more than $100 million.

- In Los Angeles, the first computer store sold assembled computers.

- "Saturday Night Live" debuted on television.

- Disposable razors were introduced.

- Arthur Ashe became the first Black American to win the Wimbledon men's single tournament.

- *Venera 9* sent pictures of the surface of Venus.

- The first cars with catalytic converters came off the assembly lines.

- The Energy Policy and Conservation Act of 1975 set import quotas on petroleum.

- Lyme disease was first discovered.

- New York City was bailed out of financial problems by the federal government.

- The U.S. merchant ship, the SS *Mayaguez*, was seized by the Khmer Rouge of Cambodia because of alleged contraband. The 39 crew members were held captive for three days. A rescue attempt authorized by President Ford resulted in the deaths of 41 American Marines.

Use the Internet and other reference sources to answer the following questions.

1. What animal was the villain in *Jaws*? _____

2. What sport did Arthur Ashe play? _____

3. What insect carries lyme disease? _____

4. Of the events listed on this page and the next page, which surprises you the most? Why?

_____

_____

_____

_____

_____

_____

Name: _____ Date: _____

How Things Have Changed

Read the statements about 1975. Add a statement about how things are the same or different today.

1. **Then:** The Altair, the first home computer based on the Z-80 microprocessor, was introduced. It had no screen or printer and came in a kit. You had to assemble the parts yourself.

   Now: _____

   _____

   _____

2. **Then:** Secretary of State John Quincy Adams recommended that the U.S. convert to the metric system in 1821. Congress legalized the metric system in 1866. After that, it became commonly used in science and medicine, but it never became popular. When the Metric Conversion Act was passed in 1975, most people ignored it.

   Now: _____

   _____

   _____

3. **Then:** Bill Gates and Paul Allen started a small company called Microsoft to produce computer software.

   Now: _____

   _____

   _____

4. **Then:** Computerized checkouts were first used in supermarkets.

   Now: _____

   _____

   _____

5. **Then:** U.S. television networks agreed to set a "family hour," free of sex and violence.

   Now: _____

   _____

   _____

Name: _____ Date: _____

That's a Big Ten-Four, Good Buddy (1976)

- CB radio popularity peaked: 656,000 CB radio applications were filed each month during 1976. Many drivers now use cell phones, but truck drivers still rely on CBs for road and weather information.

- After an 11-month journey, *Viking I* landed on Mars on July 20, 1976, and began transmitting color pictures of the Martian landscape.

- Queen Elizabeth II became the first head of state to send an e-mail message.

- The first popular microcomputer word-processing program, "Electric Pencil" was introduced.

- The Cray-1 supercomputer could handle 240 million calculations per second.

- The Ethernet was invented to speed data over coaxial cable.

- Small satellite dishes began appearing in residential backyards.

- Legionnaire's disease infected 182 and killed 29. The disease got its name because the first appearance of the flu-like disease struck at an American Legion convention in Philadelphia.

- The Supreme Court ruled that the death penalty did not constitute "cruel and unusual punishment" and was not banned by the Constitution.

- Bicentennial celebrations were held across the United States.

Use the Internet and other reference sources to answer the following questions.

1. What does CB stand for? _____

2. If you could have been the one to send the first e-mail ever, who would you have sent it to, and what would it have been about?

   _____

   _____

   _____

3. What is your opinion about the Supreme Court's decision on the death penalty?

   _____

4. Use a dictionary. Define *bicentennial*. _____

   _____

   What event was being celebrated? _____

   _____

Name: _____ Date: _____

Computers Come of Age

The first successful digital computer was completed in 1945 and weighed 60,000 pounds. Although computers became smaller and more efficient in the sixties, they were not practical for home use because they were too large and too expensive.

In 1973, you could buy the Scelbi-8H computer kit for $575 and build your own computer with a microprocessor. By 1975, you could have bought one of the first IBM portable computers, which weighed 50 pounds with 16K of memory, for $9,000, but it would have cost you $20,000 for 64K.

Two college dropouts, Steve Jobs and Steve Wozniak, changed everything in 1976 when they went to work in a garage to build the Apple I, a crude version of the personal computer. They sold 600 of the pre-assembled units for $666.60. The following year, they developed a better model, the Apple II. In great demand, the Apples were bought as fast as they could be built.

Another college dropout, Bill Gates, founded Microsoft with his partner Paul Allen. Gates had designed an operating system for IBM. His company began by selling operating system software and eventually became the largest corporation in the United States

Each year computer technology changed. Today's home computers are faster and have more memory than anything available in the seventies.

ARPANET, a system developed in the sixties, was the forerunner of today's Internet system. The Internet is often called the "Information Superhighway."

Use the Internet and other reference sources to find out more about ARPANET and the Internet.

1. Who developed ARPANET? _____

2. What was ARPANET? _____

   _____

3. Why was ARPANET developed? _____

   _____

4. Why do you think it was called ARPANET? _____

   _____

   _____

5. What do you like best about computers? _____

   _____

   _____

6. What do you like best about the Internet? _____

   _____

   _____

Name: _____ Date: _____

What Happened in 1977?

- *Star Wars* became the biggest movie hit of all time. Other movie hits were *Saturday Night Fever* and *Close Encounters of the Third Kind.*

- Atari™ introduced a programmable home video cartridge game system.

- Best-selling computers of the year were the Apple II™, Commodore Pet™, and TRS-80™.

- Nintendo™ began selling computer games.

- AT&T™ began transmitting telephone calls by fiber-optics.

- Millions mourned when they learned of the death of "the King"— King Elvis that is. Rock-and-roll idol Elvis Presley died at the age of 42.

- The United States signed treaties with Panama agreeing to hand the canal and its surrounding zone over to Panama by the year 2000.

- Funding began for the neutron bomb, an atomic weapon designed to spread radiation to kill people and leave buildings intact.

- For the first time, a woman was ordained as an Episcopalian priest.

- Magnetic Resonance Imaging (MRI) was first used to map the brain and other parts of the body.

- Son of Sam was arrested after a 12-month killing spree. He claimed the 1,000-year-old spirit of a black dog named Sam ordered him to kill people.

- The first Concorde SST left from New York City. Despite design setbacks and environmental protests, a flight route was established between New York and Paris.

- The Alaskan pipeline was completed.

- A 25-hour blackout in New York City resulted in widespread looting.

1. Use the Internet and other reference sources to find two events not listed above that occurred in 1977.

   _____

   _____

   _____

   _____

Name: _____ Date: _____

What If?

1. What if you could meet anyone who was famous during the 1960s or 1970s? Who would you most like to meet, and why?

    _____

    _____

    _____

    _____

    _____

    _____

    _____

2. What if you had been born in 1965? How do you think your childhood would have been different?

    _____

    _____

    _____

    _____

    _____

    _____

    _____

3. Write a "what if?" question about the 1960s or 1970s and answer it.

    Question: _____

    _____

    _____

    Answer: _____

    _____

    _____

    _____

    _____

Name: _____ Date: _____

News in '78

Post Office News
- The cost of mailing a letter jumped to 15 cents.

Medical News
- Louise Brown was the world's first test-tube baby.

- A procedure called balloon angioplasty was developed to treat coronary heart disease.

- Ultrasound was first used.

Communication News
- The first tests of cellular telephones were made.

- Electronic typewriters went on sale.

Entertainment News
- The comic strip "Garfield" appeared for the first time in 21 newspapers.

- Games like "Space Invaders" were popular in arcades.

- Atlantic City permitted gambling.

Yummy News
- Ben Cohen and Jerry Greenfield started their company in a renovated gas station in Burlington, Vermont.

New York City News
- A new law made it mandatory for dog owners to clean up after their pets to eliminate the approximately 40 million pounds of droppings being left by dogs in New York City each year.

Use the Internet and other reference sources to answer the following questions.

1. How much did mailing a letter cost before the increase to 15 cents? _____

2. How much does it cost today to mail a letter? _____

3. In what country was Louise Brown born? _____

4. What is ultrasound used for? _____

5. Who created "Garfield"? _____

6. In what state is Atlantic City? _____

7. What product did Ben Cohen and Jerry Greenfield make? _____

Name: _____ Date: _____

Math Facts

- During the 1960 election, John F. Kennedy received 34,227,096 popular votes and 303 electoral votes; Richard M. Nixon received 34,107,646 popular votes and 219 electoral votes.

- During the 1976 election, Gerald Ford received 240 electoral votes and Jimmy Carter received 297.

- Of the approximately 200 million TV sets in the world in 1968, 78 million were in the United States.

- If you had worked for minimum wage in 1974, you would have earned $2.30 an hour.

- In 1964, a burger, fries, and a shake would have cost you 97 cents at McDonald's.

- In 1972, *LIFE* magazine went out of business after 36 years of weekly publication.

- In May 1978, Mavis Hutchinson became the first woman to run across the United States. The 3,000-mile trek took her 69 days.

Using the information above, answer the following questions.

1. By how many popular votes did Kennedy win the election? _____

2. What percentage of the popular votes did Kennedy receive in the 1960 election?

   _____

3. What percentage of the electoral votes did Kennedy receive? _____

4. Was the percentage of electoral votes Carter received higher or lower than the percent Kennedy received? _____

5. What percent of the total number of TVs were in the United States? _____

6. How much would you have earned in 1974 for a 40-hour work week? _____

7. Would it have cost you more or less than $5.00 for five burgers, fries, and shakes?

   _____

8. How many issues of *LIFE* would have been published if one came out every week for 36 years? _____

9. On the average, how many miles did Mavis Hutchinson run each day? _____

Name: _____ Date: _____

President Jimmy Carter

Circle "F" if the statement is a fact. Circle "O" if the statement is an opinion.

F   O   1. After his father died, Carter resigned from the navy and returned home to take over the family peanut farm.

F   O   2. Farmers are hard workers.

F   O   3. Carter was elected to the state Senate and became governor of Georgia in 1970.

F   O   4. Carter was a good governor.

F   O   5. As governor, Carter worked to end segregation in Georgia and appointed Blacks to administrative positions in state government.

F   O   6. Carter wasn't well known outside his home state.

F   O   7. Carter won the 1976 election against Gerald Ford by a narrow margin.

F   O   8. Gerald Ford should have tried harder to win.

Born in Plains, Georgia, in 1924, Jimmy Carter began his education in a one-room schoolhouse. He graduated from the U.S. Naval Academy at Annapolis. While in the navy, he served on gunnery vessels and nuclear submarines. He also attended classes on nuclear physics and reactor technology.

F   O   9. The federal government had become corrupt.

F   O   10. During the campaign, Carter promised to restore morality and honesty to the federal government.

F   O   11. Carter stated that the federal government must make a "... firm commitment to pure air, clean water, and unspoiled land."

F   O   12. One of Carter's first acts as president was to grant a full pardon to everyone who had refused to fight in the Vietnam War.

F   O   13. American interference in Vietnam was morally wrong.

F   O   14. When Carter ran for reelection in 1980, he lost to Ronald Reagan.

F   O   15. Failure to resolve the Iranian hostage situation cost Carter the chance for reelection.

Name: _____ Date: _____

Hostages Taken in 1979

One of the toughest challenges Jimmy Carter faced as president was the hostage situation in Iran. When followers of Ayatollah Khomeini took control of the Iranian government, the former leader, Mohammad Reza Shah Pahlavc, fled to Mexico. Carter allowed him to come to the United States for medical treatment. In November 1979, religious Iranian militants stormed the U.S. embassy in Tehran and took 66 American hostages. Although 13 of the Americans were soon released, the other 53 remained hostage.

The militants threatened to try the hostages for crimes against Iran and execute them if found guilty unless the United States returned the Shah to Iran to stand trial. (He died in July 1980.) They also demanded an apology from the United States for acts supporting the Shah and the return of billions of dollars of Iranian assets held outside their country. Negotiations failed.

President Carter authorized a secret rescue mission. However, the rescue failed, and eight members of the rescue team were killed.

Finally, after more than a year, the hostages were freed on January 20, 1981, a few hours after Ronald Reagan became president.

Other News from 1979

- The U.S. Mint began producing the Susan B. Anthony dollar.

- Cesar Chavez, leader of the United Farmworkers Union, led a strike against California lettuce growers.

- The population of the United States was 225,055,487. Life expectancy in the United States was 73.9 years.

- Jane Byrne became the first woman elected mayor of Chicago.

- CompuServe went online.

- The Sony Walkman™ became available.

- A series of mechanical and human errors caused a near meltdown of the nuclear reactor at one of the Three Mile Island plants in Pennsylvania.

1. If you had been the president, would you have sent a rescue mission to Iran? If yes, why? If no, what would you have done instead?

_____

_____

_____

Name: _____   Date: _____

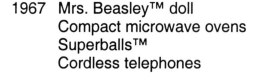

What Was New?

Circle all of the items introduced in the sixties and seventies that are no longer available. Use the Internet and other references sources.

1960 Etch-a-Sketch™
Game of Life™
ATM machines

1961 Barbie's™ boyfriend, Ken™
Carousel™ slide projector
Rock 'em, Sock 'em Robots™

1962 Lego™ building sets
Big Loo Robot™
Communications satellites
K-Mart stores
Wal-Mart stores

1963 Mousetrap™ game
ZIP codes
Pop-top cans

1964 G.I. Joe™
Easy-Bake Oven™
Ford™ Mustangs
"Jeopardy!" game show

1965 Gatorade™
Operation™ game
Battleship™ game

1966 Pampers™ disposable diapers
Silly Sand™
Fuzzy Wuzzy™ soap
Twister™ game
"Star Trek"

1967 Mrs. Beasley™ doll
Compact microwave ovens
Superballs™
Cordless telephones

1968 Spirograph™
Game of Risk™

1969 Hot Wheels™
Wizzer™ tops
"Sesame Street" show

1970 Computer floppy disks

1972 *Ms* magazine
Pong™

1973 *People* magazine
UPC barcodes

1975 Pet rocks
Mood rings
Disposable razors
Catalytic converters

1976 Apple I™ computers

1977 Apple II™ computers

1978 Electronic typewriters

1979 Sony Walkman™
Cellular telephones

1. Of the items still available, which ones do you and your family use most often?

_____

Name: _____ Date: _____

Seventies Scavenger Hunt

Use the Internet or other reference sources to find the answers to the following questions.

1. After Vice President Spiro Agnew resigned, he was later fined and sentenced to three years probation. What was the charge? _____

2. Richard M. Nixon was president from 1969 to 1974. What did the initial "M" stand for?

   _____

3. Gerald Ford became vice president while Nixon was president. When Nixon resigned, Ford became the president. Who became Ford's vice president?

   _____

4. The first strike in the history of Major League baseball took place in the 1970s. In what year did the strike take place, and how long did it last? _____

5. This pop artist best known for his works using the letters LOVE arranged in a square was commissioned by the U.S. Post Office in 1973 to design the LOVE postage stamp. What was his name? _____

6. A Supreme Court decision in 1973 protected the right to abortion. What was the name of the case? _____

7. Another important court decision in 1976 allowed the removal of life support from Karen Ann Quinlan. She had suffered severe and irreversible brain damage and had been in a coma for over a year. When her parents requested the removal of artificial life support, the hospital refused. A New Jersey Supreme Court finally ruled that the device could be disconnected, so the patient could die with dignity. When did Karen Ann Quinlan die?

   _____

8. Reggae music became popular in the United States in the seventies. Where did reggae music originate? _____

9. Before forming their own company, Apple Computers™, what companies did Steve Jobs and Steve Wozniak work for? _____

10. In 1971, Native Americans took over this former island prison, citing an 1868 treaty that allowed them to live on unoccupied land. They were protesting the U.S. government's poor record of handling treaties. What was the name of the island? _____

Name: _____ Date: _____

Read All About It!

Option 1: Read a fiction or nonfiction book about the 1960s or 1970s.
Option 2: Read a biography of someone who played a role in history during the 1960s or 1970s.
Option 3: Read one of the books that received the Newbery Award between 1970 and 1979. (See the list on the following page.) Ask your teacher if the book is appropriate before you begin.

Title and author of the book: _____

_____

Was the book fiction or nonfiction? _____

What years were covered in the book? _____

Briefly describe the main character. _____

_____

_____

Where did the main character live? _____

Summarize two major events described in the book. _____

_____

_____

_____

_____

What was the major problem the main character had to face? _____

_____

_____

_____

How was that problem resolved? If it wasn't resolved, why not? _____

_____

_____

_____

_____

Would you recommend the book to your friends? Why or why not? _____

_____

_____

The 1970s Newbery Award Winners

1979 Winner: *The Westing Game* by Ellen Raskin
Honor Book: *The Great Gilly Hopkins* by Katherine Paterson

1978 Winner: *Bridge to Terabithia* by Katherine Paterson
Honor Books: *Ramona and Her Father* by Beverly Cleary
              Anpao: An American Indian Odyssey by Jamake Highwater

1977 Winner: *Roll of Thunder, Hear My Cry* by Mildred D. Taylor
Honor Books: *Abel's Island* by William Steig
              A String in the Harp by Nancy Bond

1976 Winner: *The Grey King* by Susan Cooper
Honor Books: *The Hundred Penny Box* by Sharon Bell Mathis
              Dragonwings by Laurence Yep

1975 Winner: *M. C. Higgins, the Great* by Virginia Hamilton
Honor Books: *Figgs & Phantoms* by Ellen Raskin
              My Brother Sam is Dead by James and Christopher Collier
              The Perilous Gard by Elizabeth Marie Pope
              Philip Hall Likes Me, I Reckon Maybe by Bette Greene

1974 Winner: *The Slave Dancer* by Paula Fox
Honor Book: *The Dark Is Rising* by Susan Cooper

1973 Winner: *Julie of the Wolves* by Jean Craighead George
Honor Books: *Frog and Toad Together* by Arnold Lobel
              The Upstairs Room by Johanna Reiss
              The Witches of Worm by Zilpha Keatley Snyder

1972 Winner: *Mrs. Frisby and the Rats of NIMH* by Robert C. O'Brien
Honor Books: *Incident At Hawk's Hill* by Allan W. Eckert
              The Planet of Junior Brown by Virginia Hamilton
              The Tombs of Atuan by Ursula K. LeGuin
              Annie and the Old One by Miska Miles
              The Headless Cupid by Zilpha Keatley Snyder

1971 Winner: *Summer of the Swans* by Betsy Byars
Honor Books: *Knee Knock Rise* by Natalie Babbitt
              Enchantress From the Stars by Sylvia Louise Engdahl
              Sing Down the Moon by Scott O'Dell

1970 Winner: *Sounder* by William H. Armstrong
Honor Books: *Our Eddie* by Sulamith Ish-Kishor
              The Many Ways of Seeing: An Introduction to the Pleasures of Art
                  by Janet Gaylord Moore
              Journey Outside by Mary Q. Steele

History Projects

Complete one of these projects. Work alone, with a partner, or with a small group if appropriate.

- Create a detailed time line of the 1960s or 1970s with illustrations and maps.

- Make a videotape of an interview with a rock star or rock group of the '60s. Be sure to dress the part.

- Do a detailed comparison between any two of the men who were president in the 1960s and/or 1970s. Include the ways in which they were alike and the ways in which they were different.

- Make a scrapbook about the war in Vietnam. Add captions for all pictures. You can download pictures from the Internet, photocopy them from books, or draw your own.

- Write articles for one page of a newspaper dated any time between 1960 and 1979.

- Write and illustrate a poem about the sixties or seventies. Read your poem to the group.

- Learn and demonstrate a dance popular in the 1960s. Teach others to do the dance.

- Write a detailed report about the conditions in your city or community during the 1960s or 1970s. Include copies of local newspaper articles.

- Create a journal that could have been written by someone between 1960 and 1970 describing everyday life and events. Include at least five entries for each year.

- Prepare and present a 10-minute speech either in favor of or against the war in Vietnam.

- Prepare a detailed biography of one of the presidents or first ladies who lived in the White House during the 1960s or 1970s.

- Make a chart showing details of all important environmental events and legislation during the 1960s and 1970s.

- Do a complete history of the development of modern computers, beginning with the invention of the first analog machine by Wilhelm Schikard in 1623.

Learn More About …

Learn more about one of the people listed below who had an impact on American history during the 1960s or 1970s. Use the Internet and other reference sources to write a three- to five-page report with illustrations.

Neil Armstrong

Chubby Checker

Bella Abzug	John Glenn
Spiro Agnew	Abbie Hoffman
Edwin "Buzz" Aldrin	Grace Murray Hopper
Anna Mae Aquash	Lady Bird Johnson
Neil Armstrong	Lyndon B. Johnson
Joan Baez	Barbara Jordan
Rachel Carson	John F. Kennedy
Jimmy Carter	Billie Jean King
Cesar Chavez	Coretta Scott King
Chubby Checker	Martin Luther King, Jr.
Shirley Chisholm	Barbara McClintock
Beverly Cleary	Mickey Mantle
Bob Dylan	Roger Maris
Bobby Fischer	Thurgood Marshall
Ella Fitzgerald	Willie Mays
Peggy Fleming	Kate Millet
Gerald R. Ford	Patricia Nixon
Paula Fox	Richard M. Nixon
Aretha Franklin	Jacqueline Kennedy Onassis
Betty Friedan	Elvis Presley
	Wilma Rudolph
	Alan Shepard
	Gloria Steinem
	Maria Tallchief
	Andy Warhol

Coretta Scott King

Betty Friedan

Suggested Reading

Timelines: 1960s by Jane Duden

Timelines: 1970s by Jane Duden

An Album of the Sixties by Carol A. Emmens

20th Century Pop Culture: The '60s by Dan Epstein

20th Century Pop Culture: The '70s by Dan Epstein

Decades of the 20th Century: The 1960s From the Vietnam War to Flower Power by Stephen
    Feinstein

Decades of the 20th Century: The 1970s From Watergate to Disco by Stephen Feinstein

The Story of the Great Society by Leila M. Foster

Encyclopedia of Presidents: Lyndon B. Johnson by Jim Hargrove

The Story of Watergate by Jim Hargrove

An Album of the Seventies by Dorothy and Thomas Hoobler

Encyclopedia of Presidents: John F. Kennedy by Zachary Kent

Martin Luther King, Jr., Civil Rights Leader by Kathy Lambert

Jimmy Carter: On the Road to Peace by Caroline Lazo

Encyclopedia of Presidents: Richard Nixon by Dee Lillegard

America in the 1960s by Michael Kronenwetter

Dare to Dream: Coretta Scott King and the Civil Rights Movement by Angela Medearis

The Presidents of the United States: 1969–1990 by Ruth Oakley

20th Century Fashion: The '60s Mods & Hippies by Kitty Powe-Temperley

Encyclopedia of Presidents: Gerald Ford by Paul P. Sipiera

The Assassination of John F. Kennedy by R. Conrad Stein

The Vietnam War by Douglas Willoughby

Answer Keys

A New Decade Begins: 1960 (p. 3)
1. ATM: Automated Teller Machine

The Presidential Election of 1960 (p. 4)
1. RN	2. JFK	3. JFK
4. JFK	5. RN	6. JFK
7. JFK	8. RN	9. RN
10. RN	11. JFK	12. RN
13. BOTH	14. JFK	15. RN

Russians Lead the Space Race in 1961 (p. 5)
2. FCC: Federal Communications Commission
   FM: frequency modulation
3. Jellystone National Park

What Was New in '62? (p. 7)
1. transatlantic: across the Atlantic Ocean

ZIP into 1963 (p. 9)
1. ZIP: Zoning Improvement Program
4. Lee Harvey Oswald was the man arrested for shooting John F. Kennedy.

Dr. Martin Luther King, Jr. (p. 10)
1. segregation: separation based on race
2. civil rights: the rights to personal liberties established by the Constitution

What Happened in 1964? (p. 13)
2. transpacific: across the Pacific Ocean
3. Paul McCartney, John Lennon, George Harrison, Ringo Starr

Civil Rights Laws Passed (p. 15)
1. bigotry: prejudice against people of another race, culture, religion, etc.
3. literacy: ability to read and write
4. poll tax: fee charged for voting

"Beam Me Up, Scotty" (p. 18)
1. William Shatner and Leonard Nimoy
3. National Organization for Women

Sixties Scavenger Hunt (p. 20)
1. Ernest Evans
2. Cassius Clay
3. Charles Schulz
4. Adam West and Burt Ward
5. All were dances except the hot potato and the squash
6. Macaroni
7. Willard Scott
8. New York Jets
9. Creedence Clearwater Revival
10. Six cents

1968: A Turbulent Year (p. 23)
A. KB means kilobyte (1,000 bytes of information)
B. 1,000 KB = 1 megabyte (one million bytes)
C. 1,000 MB = 1 gigabyte (one billion bytes)

1. E	2. D	3. F
4. A	5. B	6. C

To the Moon—and Back (p. 27)
2. Michael Collins

Who's Who? (p. 29)
1. M	2. P	3. F	4. C & O
5. N	6. J	7. O	8. K
9. C	10. K	11. I	12. M
13. D	14. G	15. J	16. H & A
17. B	18. E	19. A & K	20. J
21. L	22. D		

Fashions in the Sixties (p. 30)
1. F	2. B	3. K	4. G
5. H & J	6. E	7. A	8. I
9. C	10. D	11. H	

Jeopardy (p. 31)
2. Who was John F. Kennedy?
3. What was the first moon landing?
4. Who was Martin Luther King, Jr.?
5. Who were The Beatles?
6. Who was Lyndon B. Johnson?
7. Who was Rachel Carson?

8. What was "Sesame Street"?
9. What was "Star Trek"?
10. What was the *Miranda Decision*?

What Happened in 1970? (p. 33)
1. Occupational and Safety Health Administration
3. Environmental Protection Agency

In the News in 1971 (p. 35)
3. baseball
4. chess
5. a country in southern Asia

Prices Rose in 1973 (p. 39)
1. Organization of Petroleum Exporting Countries
2. Gerald R. Ford
4. Universal Product Code

Second Battle of Wounded Knee (p. 40)
1. American Indian Movement
2. Bureau of Indian Affairs

Meet Gerald R. Ford (p. 42)
2. T   3. T   4. T   5. F
6. T   7. F   8. T   9. F
10. F

Ford Grants Pardons in 1974 (p. 43)
2. amnesty: pardon; forgiveness

What Happened in 1975? (p. 44)
1. great white shark
2. tennis
3. deer ticks

That's a Big Ten-Four, Good Buddy (1976) (p. 46)
1. citizens band
4. a 200th anniversary; occurring every 200 years; the independence of the United States in 1776

Computers Come Of Age (p. 47)
1. the Department of Defense
2. A network of computers
3. To enable universities and research organizations to exchange information

News in '78 (p. 50)
1. 13 cents
2. Answer will depend on current cost of postage.
3. England
4. Ultrasound is a medical diagnostic technique that produces a photograph or moving image to examine many parts of the body. The most common use is to examine a fetus during pregnancy.
5. Jim Davis
6. New Jersey
7. ice cream

Math Facts (p. 51)
1. 119,450   2. 50%
3. 58%   4. lower
5. 39%   6. $92
7. less   8. 1,872 issues
9. 43.5 miles

President Jimmy Carter (p. 52)
1. F   2. O   3. F   4. O
5. F   6. F   7. F   8. O
9. O   10. F   11. F   12. F
13. O   14. F   15. O

Seventies Scavenger Hunt (p. 55)
1. income tax evasion
2. Milhous
3. Nelson Rockefeller
4. 1972; 13 days
5. Robert Indiana
6. *Roe v. Wade*
7. 1985
8. Jamaica
9. Steve Jobs was a video game designer for Atari, and Steve Wozniak worked for Hewlett-Packard.
10. Alcatraz